No, My Place

Reflections on sexual harassment in Illinois government and politics

Kerry Lester
with illustrations by Pat Byrnes

ISBN:0692056564
ISBN-13:978-0692056561

To those who told us to do our best, that it would be enough.

May it be someday.

CONTENTS

INTRODUCTION

This is how it happens.

A young, ambitious woman arrives on the steps of the state Capitol, city hall or a county courthouse, heels clicking, briefcase in hand.

She's worked hard, throughout college and professional internships, to land this job.

Rock solid resume, check. Strong references, check. Game face, check.

She doesn't know it yet, but that buoyant feeling she has right now - the one tempting her to throw her hat up in the air like Mary Tyler Moore - is about to come to an abrupt end, like a pin pricking a balloon.

While she understands by now that political currency is a delicate mix of connections, favors, and power, she's still incredibly naive.

In the coming months, she'll begin to learn that the game is fixed, often putting women like herself in no-win situations.

If she keeps her head down and does her work, she's told she's too serious. If she fraternizes to develop professional relationships – be it over coffee, a business dinner, or drink – she fears rumors will begin to circulate that she's using her sexuality to curry favors.

She could be dressed conservatively, wearing a wedding or engagement ring, or frequently refer to a significant other. But still, she endures unwanted and unsolicited advances: A stray hand on her thigh or backside. Late night, liquor-fueled text messages from superiors, beginning with a casual "hey there." Innuendos and outright propositions, some so shocking that she stands there, dumbstruck, for several seconds before being able to utter a response.

If she rebuffs these, she learns, she's retaliated upon. So, she often laughs them off or stays silent, prompting the men who outnumber her in the council chamber, under the Capitol dome, or in the press box to act in the same manner toward other women without realizing their behavior is inappropriate.

After the #MeToo movement gained global attention, I was struck by the breadth and depth of harassment experienced by women working in Illinois politics and government. No newspaper or magazine piece could adequately convey the collectivity of challenges I was learning that my colleagues, mentors, and sources faced.

I'd had my own run-ins with inappropriate and sexist behavior covering politics for nearly a decade for the *Daily Herald* and the *Associated Press*. A lawmaker, over a business lunch, once remarked to me that in a marriage, "the sex just goes." A high-level campaign chief once asked me about women's orgasms. When I rebuffed a colleague's advances, he insinuated that I led him on to get ahead. At the time, I stayed quiet about it all, fearful of not being believed or damaging my own reputation.

But when a letter alleging rampant sexual discrimination at the Capitol surfaced in October 2017, I was one of more than 200 people who signed on. An editor reminded me, gently, that reporters aren't to sign on to political causes. This isn't a political cause, I remarked to him. It's an issue of civility.

In the weeks that followed, I set out to collect the stories of a diverse range of voices in various sectors of the arena. I spoke with women on both sides of the aisle as renowned and powerful as the Illinois Attorney General, Cook County State's Attorney, and Chicago City Clerk, to judges, political staffers, consultants, and former state Capitol interns.

These women of all ages, races, and backgrounds, forced to endure such treatment in order to stay in the game, signed on with a desire to finally bring their experiences to light in order to reset the rules of the often misogynistic game that is Illinois politics.

Others, still, declined the opportunity to speak out on the record, citing fears about job security or criticism from leaders and key financial backers within their own political party as the November 2018 election looms.

While the details of each woman's experience vary, a number of commonalities emerged.

While the players are different, the dynamic in many cases is quite similar. A powerful man abuses his authority in dealing with an ambitious woman. In the moment, she's often left dumbstruck, replaying the scenario in her head for months and years to follow.

In the more than two dozen interviews I conducted for this book, not a single woman who experienced harassment felt that there were appropriate mechanisms in place to report and address a problem. Sometimes, she told a superior, and the problem was ignored. Other times, she tried to handle it herself and in retaliation, her bill would be killed or a promised check for services rendered withheld. Often, she just put up with it, hoping with time, the dynamics would change.

Sick of an unwritten rule to know their place in Illinois politics and government or suffer the consequences, these brave women all signed on to this project, disclosing personal indignities in order to emphasize how commonplace harassment is, with the hope of driving change.

Here are their stories.

Kerry Lester

Angelica Alfaro, Chicago
Legislative Affairs Manager,
Chicago Department of Public Health

When the #MeToo movement started gaining ground, I realized the voice of women of color was largely missing in telling stories of harassment and discrimination.

There's a reason for that. I didn't sign the letter alleging rampant sexual harassment in Illinois.

For Latinas, for black and Asian women, for so many of us, the stakes are higher.

Harassment doesn't just happen in the political world. For me, it happened while I was in college, when I was a waitress and a bartender, and again throughout my years working at City Hall and in Springfield.

And neither age nor advancement nor success seems to change that.

A few months after I lost a 2016 primary bid for the Illinois Senate, I went to say hello to an elected official at a big political event.

As I was walking away, he slapped my ass. Hard.

At first, I felt frozen. Then – I still don't know what caused me to do it – but I grabbed his wrist and I pulled him toward me. Forcefully. I looked him straight in the eye and said, "Never fucking do that again."

At first, there was a glazed look in his eyes. He didn't process it. And then when he did, he began to laugh it off.

I've struggled with this scene, and I've replayed it often. In the moment, I felt like I did what I needed to do, but it was met by someone who treated it like a joke. What did it even mean for me to stand up for myself?

A few months later, I began to consider running for office again in 2018. I was having conversations with different elected officials, telling them about my last race, telling them about my polling numbers, and asking for their support this time around.

One lawmaker offered me a glass of wine at our business meeting, which sometimes happens. But I wasn't flirting with him. It was a professional meeting.

Yet, when he walked me out of his office, he kissed me as he said goodbye. Again, I felt frozen. This time, I didn't say anything. We don't know what goes on internally sometimes in those moments.

This behavior is inappropriate, but it's become so commonplace.

Women – myself included – too often tend to shrug it off with the same reaction. "Ah, it's a part of the culture." That doesn't make it right.

In order to really change the culture, women need to have a seat at the table. They need to stay at the table, and bring in more women alongside them. We need to be in that room. We need to run, to go through the experience and be part of the conversation. It changes the culture in the same way that diversity matters so much.

Aviva Bowen, Oak Park
Communications Director, Illinois
Federation of Teachers

There is so much attention right now on sexual assault and serial abusers, and rightfully so.

A former city councilman forcibly kissed me in a bar once.

"Oh yeah, he'll do that," I was told.

A campaign manager described one of his sexual experiences in nauseating detail and asked if it turned me on. We were driving. I couldn't leave.

But I've also endured what many call "microaggressions" in my career. These aren't the unique, stand-out events, but rather the daily experiences and sexist slights that add up.

A board member routinely asked me - and never a man of equal seniority - to make copies and coffee.

A male colleague once called me a communications "skirt."

Another referred to me as an "iron-fisted bitch." It was a compliment, he said. "Relax." I did not relax. That tends not to work.

When I inquired further at that job, I learned that people speculated that a man had ghost-written some emails for me, because I had been so assertive, for a woman. That's why "bitch" was a compliment, I guess. I looked at what I had written, and all I saw was a professional communication that lacked emojis or sentences that started demurely with, "I'm sorry, I may be totally wrong, but...".

That was a "whoa" moment for me. I realized what's expected is for women to diminish themselves. And I started thinking that lack of respect and harassment and assault were like a big pyramid.

The base of it, the part that touches the most lives and most people are familiar with is a constant lack of equal treatment for women as individuals and professionals by those who have more power.

More glaring instances of harassment would be the next level up. And at the very top is sexual assault. But all of this stems from a base of disrespect for women.

How do we change the dynamic? We tell our stories. We seize this moment and call it out. We push for change. We believe women.

And as a new mom, I'd have to say helping young girls build confidence early on is critical too, because the world will tell her she's less than a boy. Putting more women in powerful positions is important as well. Organizations and institutions have to change both culture and policy; paid leave is a great example.

I appreciate allies who stand up for what's right. We need men to contribute to Planned Parenthood and march with us. But are they also calling out their buddy on the barstool next to them and saying, "dude, that's not how you talk about a woman"? Or are they standing up in the boardroom asking why there aren't any women at the table or letting the ones who are speak without being interrupted?

If we're really talking about big picture change then it's going to have to take some sacrifice and some discomfort, from all of us. It's not easy, but it's past time.

Melinda Bush, Grayslake
Illinois State Senator

I'm clear about the inappropriate advances many of my female friends and colleagues have endured in Springfield. But I'm in my 60s; my experience has been much more about being treated in an inferior way because I'm a woman.

I've been adapting my behavior to adhere to these unwritten and unfair rules of patriarchy since I was in my 20s, when I learned to swear like a truck driver. I worked for a manufacturing company then. It was what I needed to do to fit in with the guys.

Springfield has its own set of rules for women. You don't stay out past 10 p.m. You don't get in a car alone with a man. You don't put yourself in certain situations. Even if you follow them, there's this lack of respect for us.

I've noticed when I stand and speak on the Senate floor, some of the male leaders in the chair will roll their eyes, like "just sit down, already." In caucus, a man could repeat the same thing as another man who spoke before him. Still, he gets listened to. But when a woman is seeking recognition, men feel free to cut her off and interrupt her.

I went to Senate President John Cullerton last year and told him how marginalized I feel here as a woman.

He asked, "Do I do it?"

"Absolutely," I said "When you say we have a 'crop of outstanding women lawmakers,' that's sexist. Nobody ever says we have a crop of outstanding men."

I find I really have to force my way in on the more hard-line issues, like taxation or economic development. Female lawmakers are otherwise steered toward early childhood and education legislation. We're told they're "women's issues."

So many women here are mothers, and women do have maternal tendencies. I think the male leaders see us as being softer because of that. But I know being a mom is not about being soft. I hope I raised my son to know that women are just as powerful as men.

I sponsored the bill that created the Illinois Sexual Assault Task Force, which I'm also serving on. More than anything, I hope it starts to shift the Capitol culture, that it makes men look at themselves and learn from what they're hearing. And, I'm so hopeful that this helps to pave the way for the younger women out there today, to be who they are and be sexual beings, but not have to worry their sexuality changes their ability to do their jobs.

Becky Carroll, Chicago
Political consultant

Politics is an industry where you live and die by the relationships you have.

But there's a double standard when it comes to our behavior.

I've learned personally that women have to constantly second guess a man's intent in a professional setting or decline opportunities to build relationships.

I first learned this when I was in my late 20s, when I was working on a statewide campaign. I had gotten to know a downstate Democratic County chairman whom I held in very high regard. He was incredibly cordial and helpful and insightful. I considered him a mentor.

One evening, we were at my candidate's event, and we happened to leave at the same time.

He was staying at the Chicago Athletic Association, and I didn't live far from there. We walked down Michigan Avenue, chatting as we always had. And as we reached the hotel, he asked me if I'd like to come up to his room for a nightcap. He made a specific point of noting he was staying alone, that his wife wasn't with him. He'd been married for many years.

I recall trying to process it. He was married, and many decades older than me. Politically, he was very experienced, very respected.

At that moment, I suddenly felt compromised. I simply said, "oh, thanks. I appreciate it, but I have to get up early tomorrow."

Afterward, I remember feeling ... bad. Did I do something to indicate that I wanted something more than just conversation? I made a point afterward to never have a conversation with him again. I was embarrassed.

A few years after that, I was working for the City of Chicago.

A tomboy with three brothers growing up, I naturally developed a lot of great relationships with the men that I worked with, among them the guy to whom I reported. We connected politically, ideologically, and we liked a lot of the same things.

It was a platonic friendship I would have had with a man or a woman. One night after work, we were out watching a game at a bar. I remember walking out into the street when he leaned in and kissed me.

I immediately said something along the lines of, "What the hell? I'm not interested. You need to go home." He knew I had a boyfriend. And I never, in any way, showed that kind of interest.

After that, our professional relationship eroded as well. When I was being considered for another role, he began to say my work was sub-par, when it had been praised before. I didn't get the job.

I thought, "ok, this is how it works. If I rebuff you, this is what happens. I get blackballed."

I didn't choose to report anything because people would say, "why were you out drinking with him?" If I were a guy, nobody would have questioned it.

To this day, he's working in government someplace else, and I'm going out of my way to avoid him. It's not painful; I'm just angry.

After the Harvey Weinstein revelations came out, I decided to work on changing the culture in Illinois. I was shocked by how many stories many of my friends had.

Women need to know that if they come forward, we have their backs.

Cristina Castro, Elgin
Illinois State Senator

What's frustrating to me is that there are a number of lawmakers in Illinois that just want this issue of sexual harassment to die. It's both men and women from both parties.

Some women don't want to go too far, because they're afraid it will hurt their chances to get leadership positions. Come on. This is a national problem.

Recently in Springfield, I've asked myself, "what are we doing down here? Are we serious, or are we just playing lip service to the issue?"

I'm sensitive to the problem of harassment – which is really taking advantage of someone – because I watched my Hispanic parents who spoke little English be taken advantage of and not know where to turn. You learn from that. Their experiences molded me and pissed me off.

Women experience sexual harassment in a lot of different ways. During my time working in marketing and communications at Elgin Community College, I remember hearing stories from girls and telling them they needed to say something, to draw a firm line. But there's often a fear of retaliation that holds people back.

In learning about the state's new anti-harassment legislation, some of my colleagues have gotten freaked out in training because they talked about stuff you needed to report.

"Can I get sued?" has been one of the most common, and disgusting, questions.

This is a culture that has been cultivated for decades. It's a culture we need to systematically start to change. It's going to take time, and we need to start somewhere. We need to continue to keep the pressure on.

It means that as members of the General Assembly need to start looking at the working conditions for those who serve. We need to make sure that those who come to the people's house feel safe, and feel comfortable. We need to be appropriate.

We need to look at harsher punishments and legislation that holds lawmakers to the same standards as everybody else, including under the Human Rights Act. Everyone needs to go through training.

If we can't do this, that puts a lot of good people who go down there for the right reasons in a bad light.

I don't want people to say things are never going to change.

Katelynd Duncan, Chicago
Political consultant, Democratic
fundraiser

I took two years off of college to work on Barack Obama's 2008 presidential campaign. I loved every minute of it. Later, when I graduated, I wanted to stay in politics but didn't want to live in Washington, D.C. I saw a need for fundraising here in Illinois and decided to open up my own consulting firm.

At the time I was traveling around the state to teach local politicians how to build a federal-style fundraising operation. Sometimes, I'd meet clients at their homes.

One of my first clients was a young member of the Chicago City Council who made it very clear to me that he found me attractive. Every time I came to his house the lights would be low; he'd have beers out, and there would be music playing. I had all of these binders with me, but my work was constantly being interrupted by propositions from him. I would decline, telling him that I wasn't interested and had a boyfriend.

Eventually, it came time for him to pay me for my work. I sent him a text that I needed to get a check from him. He told me to come to his office, and when I arrived, he asked me again, "When are we going to go out?" I declined for like the hundredth time.

And then he said, "I don't have a check for you."

It took me a year to get the money I earned.

That same year, I had a client - a state legislator - who would repeatedly try to reach me at midnight and first thing on Saturday mornings. He was being extremely aggressive with me. I told his campaign manager in writing that he was making me uncomfortable, and I wanted him to stop.

She said there was nothing she could do about it, and I countered by saying, "I don't know what to tell my boyfriend when I receive these inappropriate calls and texts on Saturday nights."

That was it. As soon as I used the word "inappropriate," I was fired immediately.

I feel like I was treated this way at the time because I was on my own, starting my own business with no powerful allies who could create repercussions. These lawmakers were in a position of power, and I was not.

I'm 31 now and want to work in politics for a long time, but I find myself wondering how I will react when it happens again, and I'm sure it will.

That's part of why I decided to work on the Illinois Say No More movement. Speaking out is an opportunity to make it easier for all of us to navigate the waters of a brutal industry.

Katharine Eastvold, Springfield
Former spokeswoman, Illinois Senate
Democrats

I've always had reasons to stay quiet about it.

Among them: It wasn't as bad for me as for some women. The male senators I staffed and male superiors to whom I reported were nothing but respectful toward me; I wouldn't want to make things difficult for them by complaining about other men.

If I spoke up, I might appear easily offended and hard to work with, known more for my feminism, less for my policy expertise and writing ability. It might be harder to be taken seriously and transcend my gender for the sake of the team and the public good.

But while the harassment and differential treatment I experienced was minor compared to what many other women suffered, the fact is that I, too, worked within a culture that forced women to surmount additional barriers to success.

I consider myself lucky, however. I didn't have to work closely with the legislator who grabbed me from behind at the end-of-session party in May 2013. I'd also spent most of the party discussing policy matters in an entirely professional manner with a senator whom I did staff.

The following year was no different. The lawmaker who walked up behind me and rubbed my back while I was discussing a press release with one of his colleagues on the Senate floor likewise had no power over me. Afterwards, I gave him a stern look, and it never happened again.

The frequent comments on my looks or admonitions from lobbyists, doorkeepers, and other Capitol denizens to "smile; you'll look prettier" didn't stop me from doing my job.

Still, they were challenges my male colleagues, for the most part, did not have to face. This double standard is wrong and unfair, and it serves poorly the people of Illinois who count on a working state government. So, I'm no longer ashamed or afraid to speak about it.

Sara Feigenholtz, Chicago
Illinois State Representative

You don't get infinite chances to get things right. I believe that, and that's the moment we're in right now in terms of changing the culture at the state Capitol and in Illinois politics.

I was sexually harassed in my 20s, by a man who outranked me on a campaign I was working on. As an elected lawmaker, I've seen firsthand, the power imbalance, the patriarchy, in Springfield, for more than 20 years. I've also become very protective of younger women who work in politics, who have come to me and confided in me about their experiences.

To me this is so much more than just about sexual harassment. It's about what happens when people, mostly men, want to leverage their power over you to influence you. And that gets very gray in Springfield, because it's people's job to convince you to vote for something that might not otherwise be something you'd support.

With time, I've realized, I can't control others. I can only control my feelings and myself.

About five years ago, I actually went out and started getting personal coaching about how to handle abusive behavior at the Capitol. I have learned to put a barrier up, to literally look at these people and say, "Stop it." If people are abusive to me, I now call out that behavior in public.

We don't have a human resources department in Springfield. There are no checks and balances in the caucuses, or within the executive branch offices. And so this effort to change the culture down there is really a belts and suspenders effort.

Right now, there are a lot of conversations going on behind the scenes by women, who are coalescing. We're trying to figure out how to transition out of the environment we have right now in Springfield, and what the new normal should look like. And we're trying to do that at the same time some of the legislature's most powerful females. like Majority Leader Barbara Flynn Currie, have announced plans not to seek re-election.

In addition to legislation requiring harassment training, we need to figure out how women in Springfield can empower themselves and not just skulk away. I'm tired of bitching about it. That said, there's a fine line between cupcake and bitch.

Fear of retaliation is the next frontier. Sabotaging someone at work is a passive form of harassment and abuse. It's something we need to decide how to deal with.

Kim Foxx, Chicago
Cook County State's Attorney

The main reason I ran for this office was to change its environment. Of course I wanted to do justice and all of those great things, but I wanted to come back, and really work on dismantling the culture I had watched chew up and spit out women for 12 years.

In workplaces like this, you endure things you shouldn't have to. You do what you've got to do. You toughen your skin; you build a callous.

Throughout my life - growing up, in college, working - I've been cat-called. It's an atmosphere you get used to, about what it means to be a woman and sexualized. But that in itself is different than workplace harassment, where people have authority and power over you. That's ultimately what led me to quit my job here as an assistant state's attorney.

I had a supervisor when I worked in juvenile court, when I was in my early 30s.
And he was very affable, very warm, took a shine to my work. He told me I had the bones of a really great trial lawyer.

But he would often say inappropriate things to other men about women he came in contact with on the job. Witnesses. Other attorneys. He'd say dumb shit, like "I could do discovery on her."

One day, a group of us was trying to figure out where to go to lunch. The suggestion was a beef place that had the same first name as his. And he looked at me, thrusted, and says to me, "Yeah, you like that Italian beef, don't you?" We were on an elevator with a bunch of guys from our office.

I didn't want to demonstrate that I was embarrassed in front of others. It was one of those things where you start to think that saying something might make people ask, "Can't she take a joke? Is she too uptight?"

I remember being really disappointed in myself that I didn't have a better comeback, that I only laughed, a little. I thought I would try to go along with the joke instead of being the butt of the joke.

He stayed around until he got caught leaving another woman a really vulgar, obnoxious voicemail. But the person doing that investigation? He was somebody who used to joke about who I must have slept with to get a slot teaching at a national academy.

I had a judge, when I was seven months pregnant, call and tell me how sexy I was. On voicemail. But everyone knew him, so I laughed it off.

When I rose to become a supervisor though, I felt a tremendous amount of responsibility for the women who were under my supervision.

We had a chief in our division who was known for everything from literally looking up women's skirts to saying he wanted his own pretty, female intern, to asking a young woman about giving blow jobs.

And so I lobbied to get this guy fired. Problem was, he was very good friends with the former state's attorney.

He retired at the end of 2012. Everyone had to attend his farewell party, even though we hated him. And the state's attorney was there. She gets up and speaks and is tearfully saying what a good man he is! And it was in that moment that I knew nothing was ever going to change there. It's a fruitless effort when the boss knows the predator and says, "he's a good dude." That was it for me, and even though he was retiring, I knew I couldn't work for her, or work there, any longer.

The court culture is really bad. Harassment is allowed to fester here, because you're talking about legitimate power, like your client's sentence.

If a judge is hitting on you, and you piss him off, what happens to your clients? The stakes are really high.

I will tell you, even though I'm relatively protected now because I'm the boss, I know there are people sitting in courthouses where my attorneys go every day, who are still behaving inappropriately, and I am mortified. But I don't know what happens when I start pointing fingers, and saying "it's him, it's him, it's him." I am still scared.

There's an apprehension to changing behavior around here. For many who have worked here a long time, there's a sense of "this is who we are."

I wrestle with how to handle this a lot. I recently had a bureau chiefs meeting where we talked through a series of #MeToo stories. And I asked them, "Who here doesn't think that we have a culture problem?" A number of men came up to me afterwards, and said, "I've never thought about it from the perspective of a woman, or a black person." Because we also have racial issues.

There's this fear that benign behavior is going to be misconstrued. But what people fail to realize is that behavior is not benign.

One of the problems I encountered when trying to report things was having to do so with an ally of the offender. So over the summer, we revised our sexual harassment policy. And I hired an ethics officer.

I've also intentionally hired a lot of women to work in top administrative posts. I wanted to make sure that I considered a woman for every spot. And it so happened that the women I chose were the best qualified for the work.

Yet, there is a skepticism about what I'm doing. People are like, "Oh my gosh, you're hiring all these women, you're hiring all these black people." They never ask that question of men. You see a male cabinet with one or two token women, and no one's ever like, "that's bad." Why does it become a thing when a woman is in charge and the tables are turned?

I talk about this all the time with my two daughters, who are 14 and 11.

When I was running for state's attorney, I told them that I'd be working really hard and not around much for a few months. When they asked why, I told them that when Mommy worked there, there were things that happened to the women there. I explained that men who were in positions of power were using that power to get what they wanted.

As my daughters have gotten older, and as my oldest has gone to high school, I think it's my obligation to talk to them about what it means to be a woman - how people are going to look at you, how they will judge you. I'd rather tell them too much as opposed to too little. I'd rather they be over-informed. I want them to say, "that's not OK."

Robyn Gabel, Evanston
Illinois State Representative

In the late 1990s, I was a lobbyist attending an event at a bar near the Capitol in Springfield. It was a Monday night fundraiser, the kind some hold the day before session starts for the week.

I was seated at one end of a long, outside table and talking to another lobbyist who sat down next to me. He was a former House Majority leader. He started the conversation.

"Remember that time you came into my office and said you wanted to have sex with me?" he asked. "I said no then, but now I say yes."

I told him, "No, that wasn't me. I never said that." But he refused to believe me, and he repeated the story again.

I insisted again. "No, it absolutely wasn't me," I said. "I went to Barbara Flynn Currie for help on legislation. I always go to her, because she's the woman in leadership."

Then he looked at me, looked at my chest, and said, "Oh my god. Those are the biggest nipples I've ever seen. They look like pencil erasers."

I tried to shrug it off, saying "that's what God gave me." I thought that would be the end of it.

But then he shouted the same comment to men down at the other end of the table. At that point, I was so humiliated, I got up and walked out.

After that night, I encountered him from time to time. I would see him in the Capitol, and he was embarrassed. He would not look me in the eye.

I didn't report him. I didn't confront him. But he also never apologized.

Fast forward 20 years, and things have changed for me. First of all, I'm that much older. Secondly, I'm a lawmaker. But what I hear from younger female lobbyists is that things haven't changed at all.

I feel like it's our job as legislators to pass laws that will help change the culture. We cannot physically change people's minds, but we can create an atmosphere where that kind of behavior is not tolerated.

We have to do it through consequences, so there not only has to be a place to report, but people also need to be called out. There have to be fines. Public humiliation - of the offenders, not the victims - is what will be an impetus for change.

Lisa Madigan, Chicago
Illinois Attorney General

Sexual harassment is an aggressive and pernicious form of sex discrimination that until now, society has done little to stop.

I experienced harassment early and often, and in many different forms - through unwelcome comments, advances, touching, and stalking. It started at a surprisingly early age.

My response has been different based on the circumstances. I ignored cat-calls walking down LaSalle Street as a young teenager. When inappropriate and uncomfortable comments were made to me at political events I attended with my parents, I moved to a different part of the room. When, as a state senator, a man would come to my office or serial call my phone and leave 30, 40, 50 messages a day, I snuck around the Capitol to try and avoid him. Eventually, I reported him to law enforcement.

No woman is unaffected by this. I'm well aware of the fact that anything I've endured just pales in comparison to the constant onslaught many women, particularly lower income women of color, are subjected to.

I'm 51. I'm in a generation of women who's the daughter of a mother who worked incredibly hard outside the home, who opened up the world to a lot of new opportunities for me. When I was young, I watched my single mom in the workplace as a receptionist at a law firm. I remember when her firm hired its first female lawyer. That was exciting for me and the women who worked there.

So, I grew up around lawyers, with the mindset that I should get as much education as possible, to achieve as much as possible. I knew that women in my generation were lucky to have the chance to sit in those seats, to get the jobs. Twenty years ago, I wasn't at the point of speaking out about sexual harassment when it was happening.

As a female elected official, you're cognizant that you've become a role model. There were times when I would be in my state Senate office on Addison Street in the late 1990s and mothers and fathers would come in with their little girls to introduce them to me, to show them that serving as an elected official was possible for girls.

When I became Illinois Attorney General, my experiences with harassment virtually disappeared. Power does change the dynamic. And in this office, I've put women in significant leadership positions, including the first female chief of staff and head of the criminal division. The office has become more female. It's a place where everyone's welcome, and everyone's voices are heard.

When some of my female lawyers and staff members have left to go to the private sector, I hear about how different their new workplace culture is.

"You have no idea what it's like out there," they say, telling me about the dirty jokes and comments that are made to them.

My daughters are ages 13 and 9. They're growing up at a time when the conversation about harassment is happening publicly. It's something we talk about at home.

Last year, we went to the women's march together and my oldest made a sign that said, "We don't just do pretty." They're very aware of sexism, and all the cultural messaging that takes place, from grocery store magazines to inappropriate clothes to music videos.

We are now seeing a group of women coming of age whose mothers and fathers told them they can do anything. When they've gotten into the world, they found it to be very different. It wasn't welcoming; it wasn't fair.

They're the ones who showed up and refused to accept the status quo.

I believe a culture change will come from the awareness that all women, even successful women that have gotten in a position of power endure this. And the recognition that we won't continue to tolerate it.

Theresa Mah, Chicago
Illinois State Representative

Several years ago, before I was a lawmaker, I was an advocate down in Springfield working on a bill. When the legislation finally passed both chambers, a state representative who had helped me suggested we go to The Globe, a popular bar near the Capitol, and celebrate.

It was then when I experienced how gross and entitled many men can be. While we were having drinks, this lawmaker became very handsy. He was clearly not being professional and took the instance as a sexual opportunity. He was on the make, and it became obvious to me that this was pretty habitual for him.

After he'd had a few drinks, he put his hand on my leg and invited me up to his room. I was able to extricate myself from the situation as quickly and politely as possible. I made it clear that I wasn't interested and left it at that. I was glad that the bill we had worked on together had passed already, so I didn't really have to have much to do with him after that. I was able to put that episode behind me.

I think a lot of men in Springfield behave like that because they believe it's the norm, and they don't believe there's any chance they'll be reprimanded or anything. And experiences like mine aren't serious enough that most women would go and report them. I didn't.

There are all kinds of stories like mine floating around Springfield. Sometimes offenders are named, sometimes they're not. But there's a permeating sense of entitlement. Some people feel Springfield is some kind of sexual playground and don't wear their wedding rings when they're there.

Some people are fine with it. They see it as part of the job. I'm not going to judge, but it's a power dynamic I prefer not to be in.

If more women get into positions of power, this is all less likely to happen.

Karen McConnaughay, St. Charles
Illinois State Senator

The test for women in politics is always the same: It's the question of, "Does she have the guts to push back and play hardball?"

When I became Kane County's first female board chairwoman, I felt very tested by the male colleagues in government who were my equals. I had to prove myself more and differently than they did. That was the culture for women coming up at the time.

I knew I had to make it crystal clear that I was every bit as capable as they were. I learned to take on this defensive mode, to communicate that I wasn't to be messed with.

I showed that I was not backing down, showed that I wasn't there just to do what I was told. And in the end, I felt I earned the respect of male officials, many of whom have been incredibly respectful of me to this day.

Yet, I look at young women coming up behind me and remember those trials I went through decades ago. I knew if I wanted to get ahead I would have to suck things up, not dwell on disrespectful and inappropriate behavior. That is just unacceptable. Women should never have to put up with that.

I sit on the Legislative Ethics Commission. In late 2017, I learned that there were 27 pending ethics complaints but no investigations, due to the lack of an inspector general in the role. There was no hesitation on my part about speaking up about that.

I've pushed for an independent inspector general, because the Ethics Commission needs to stand independent of the General Assembly's meddling.

The process itself was designed to protect the accused, not the accuser. It has become very apparent the General Assembly cannot police itself. This entire process needs to be removed from the General Assembly and leadership's control.

Women at the Capitol do not feel that their voices will be heard on issues of harassment, that justice will be served or that anything will be done about it.

I don't think about my work on the issue in terms of being a Republican woman in the legislature.

This is simply a conversation that was long overdue. I feel that I owe it to all women. I value the mentorship I received from other women as I went through my own career in government in the last 27 years. I look at how I want the world to be for my two daughters and five granddaughters.

This is not just an opportunity to change attitudes and behaviors and culture because of what's going on. It's an obligation.

Josina Morita, Skokie
Commissioner, Metropolitan Water
Reclamation District

I've had a range of jobs, from running a nonprofit to working as a policy advocate down in Springfield, to running for office and now serving as an elected official.

For me, the worst experience has been as a candidate and how you get treated by elected officials and committeemen in the Democratic Party's political structure. You're in a public position, and people know you're asking for something. And harassment is the ultimate expression of power.

I was the first Asian American to be endorsed by the Cook County Democratic Party. Racism and sexism were very intertwined here in my experience. In part out of curiosity, people tested boundaries.

I'd greet an elected official at an event, and he'd make a comment about my eyes. He'd put his hand on my lower back. Some were mayors, aldermen, or party officials, and some were state lawmakers.

"I've never tasted Chinese pussy before," one party committeeman told me at a crowded political event in 2013. I was shocked. I looked around, and it was one of those things where you almost question your own hearing. He said it in passing. And by the time I was coming to, he was already gone. It's a weird time warp when that happens. I wondered, should I chase him down and yell at him? But by the time you process it, it's over.

The hardest part for me is that this behavior surprised me. When I was beginning in politics, no one ever pulled me aside and said, "this might happen to you."

Now, when I speak to women, I say, "I hope this doesn't happen to you, but I have never experienced sexism or racism as explicitly as I did on the campaign trail." My biggest suggestion for them is to be prepared.

I tell them, "Know what you want to say. Know what you want to do in a situation. Know your options."

As a woman who has run for office, I now feel a responsibility to give other women my best advice. I feel a responsibility to tell them the things I wish someone had told me.

Kristal Rivers, Chicago
Judge, Cook County Circuit Court

I was 21 years old and a freshman at Drake Law School. I had a professor who would literally watch my breasts as I walked across the classroom. He would stop what he was doing and stare at me.

I sat in the front row, and he would gyrate in front of my desk. I couldn't move. There wasn't any other seat.

One day, I was in the library bent over a desk when he came up behind me and put his entire body weight on top of my backside. He hugged me and told me I did so well in class. He squeezed me and grinded up against my body.

It was 20 years ago, and I feel like it was yesterday. I can still feel his hot breath in my ear.

I thought I was the only one who noticed all of this. But then I went to a law school party and a number of my classmates told me they saw it too.

I stopped coming to class, and I was punished. He changed my final exam grade from a B to a much lower grade, one I knew I didn't deserve.

Soon after that exam, I went to another male professor and told him what happened. I asked him what I needed to do about it.

He said, "Kristal, you're a first-year law student. People stick together here. If you told on him, other professors may hold it against you."

I have been mad at myself for years for not doing anything more in that situation. I knew it wasn't my fault, but I was too afraid of not being believed. How do you prove that somebody watches your breasts every time you walk into a classroom?

Sexual harassment makes you question who you are. I know I can fight like a dog for another human being, but when it comes to fighting for myself, am I going to back down?

I've had a good career and wonderful jobs. But still, as a lawyer, I have ultimately felt like my worth has been devalued because I was a woman.

We cannot let this become an issue of the moment and hope it's healed. We have to say "no more" every single, solitary time - no more to boys pulling girls' pigtails, no more to saying a man can't control himself when he gets excited.

Caitlin Rydinsky, Pawnee
Former Public Affairs Reporting
Intern, Illinois Issues magazine

During a time when more and more women are coming forward with experiences of sexual harassment and abuses of power, I find it uncanny that so many of us can relate to those situations and empathize with those individuals.

Studying for an undergraduate degree at Western Illinois University, I always knew that I wanted to sit opposite lawmakers and question them as a reporter.

It took me four years to work up the courage to go back to school for my master's and gain a seat in the press box. Little did I know what that experience was going to bring – an entirely new education in the inappropriate relations between interns, staffers and reporters with lawmakers and lobbyists.

Adding a twist to all this, early on during my internship, I found out I was pregnant. I went through those life changes as a woman, during a prominent election year.

Working in tight quarters with reporters cramming around lawmakers and candidates is awkward enough; adding a growing belly just increased the sense of feeling uncomfortable about my condition.

To compensate, I learned to approach interviews as an efficient task rather than a conversation, a different style than many other reporters used, or than I was taught. Still, inappropriate comments and questions came.

One lawmaker suggested I was biased when I was reporting on legislation that would have prohibited pregnancy discrimination in the workplace. I frequently found it alarming that grown men were unable to keep their eyes off my stomach and chest in a professional setting.

At the same time, because I was pregnant, I was able to see the close relations that lawmakers had with staffers and interns from a clear and sober lens.

While it was necessary to have connections with lawmakers as a reporter in order to gain access to information, I found it unnerving how some of the lawmakers would communicate with reporting interns and General Assembly staffers. They were grown, married men, contacting students at bars and via late night text messages.

Growing up as a woman, you learn that individuals will gawk at a woman for what she is wearing. Somehow, we've been taught to think this is acceptable, that it's something to be ignored unless you want to lessen your chances of achieving your career goals.

At first, I was hesitant to speak up about my situation. Why should I speak of circumstances that happened years ago, I wondered?

But the more I thought about it, the more I felt it was important to for those who have stayed silent about this behavior, because it's become so normalized. We have become far too numb to the issue.

Anna Valencia, Chicago
Chicago City Clerk

People took a chance on me, by giving opportunities to a young Latina from Granite City.

I want to pay that forward, and use my position as a platform to help women advance, to make sure working in government and politics is a viable, fulfilling option for them.

Working as a communications staffer in the state Senate in my mid-20s, I saw how separate rules really inhibit women from getting ahead.

The profession is all about relationship building, sometimes in social settings.

But during my first legislative session, an older, female colleague pulled me aside and said, "Do not go out to the bars after session. Do not go out with the senators. Go straight home. You do not want to be labeled a slut."

And that stuck with me, so I did what she advised. But I also kept my head down, and didn't speak up about all the slut shaming that went on down there. I regret that when I think about it now.

A few weeks ago, a writer from the student newspaper at Columbia College came to interview me, as a Chicagoan she admired.

She asked me how I responded when people made comments about my looks, or said inappropriate things. And I told her that I generally thank people for the compliment, or navigate around the situation.

Thinking about it more after the interview, I realized, I hate that answer. Women shouldn't have to brush things off anymore.

So many women get disillusioned, because men do not like women coming into their spaces, and they box them out. Working in Mayor Rahm Emanuel's office as his legislative director, I noticed a number of city officials who blatantly bypass a woman so they can work with a man instead.

You would be surprised that when I needed to have a spot filled, people would tell me, "Make sure you have a white man on your Springfield team." And that was infuriating, that sending a diverse team of women was not enough.

To really make a movement, we not only need more seats at the table and in leadership, but we need true male allies who are going to stand with us in meetings and are going to speak up when something isn't appropriate. I've been blessed to have some of those figures in my career, both in Senate President John Cullerton and Mayor Rahm Emanuel's offices.

We don't have the power to remove elected officials, unless they resign, and especially in Springfield, that's not going to happen.

We have to call them out, and get past the fear of retaliation.

AFTERWORD

<u>No My Place in an Era of Say No More</u>

2017 was the Year of the Silence Breakers. Across the country, women from all industries came forward with their experiences of misogyny and harassment in the workplace. Their stories ranged from the daily aggressions to the criminal invasion of one's body. Through the bravery of countless women, a few things became abundantly clear.

This happens to every woman, in every industry, in some way. If it were not for geography and socioeconomics, it would be very difficult to distinguish between the experience of a woman in Hollywood from that of a woman on the Hill or an hourly wage worker at a local hotel. Women are denied the ability to thrive in the workplace, blocked from opportunities for advancement, forced to operate in conditions where their very safety is at stake. It is impossible for anyone to reach their full potential in such an environment.

The seemingly innocuous comments and unsolicited touches cannot be ignored. Many headlines have focused on the salacious details of the crimes allegedly committed by the Weinsteins, the Lauers, and the Moores of the world. While rightfully feeling outraged on behalf of their victims, the question must be asked: how were men like these allowed to maintain positions of power and authority for so long? It's a clear indicator of a dysfunctional culture that spans many industries. This is fostered by the tolerance of the casual and inappropriate touching and "jokes" about the appearance of a female colleague. Every time a man is allowed to objectify a woman, it signals that such behavior is not only tolerable, but perfectly acceptable. To a predator, it is permission to treat women as objects that exist solely for their pleasure. We must make it clear - there will be consequences.

Society has come a long way in a very short time. And yet there is a longer road ahead. It's true - there *is* much progress to acknowledge: this movement has sparked critical dialogues, passed legislation, and seen the creation of task forces in both the public and private sectors. These are all steps in the right direction. But the early wins do not mean that women and their allies can sit back and celebrate. While some may feel that the boxes have been checked and business as usual can resume, it's important to maintain vigilance. Elected officials must be held accountable for creating lasting systemic change that will leave Illinois' most important institutions indelibly changed for the greater good.

2018 is undoubtedly the Year of the Woman. We must show up for the cause, committed to creating space for *all* women - inclusive of all racial, ethnic, religious, economic, and sexual identities. We must be prepared to stand shoulder to shoulder with one another as we move this work forward. We must continue to say, "No more." And, to truly change behavior and culture, we must continue to demand more women be at the table in positions of leadership across industries and for more men to be allies in this fight.

Let us all be inspired by the courage and wisdom contained in these pages, and may we each embody a bit of the spirit of the women who shared their stories, and many of those who did not. Every time we know we belong but are made to feel as though we don't, every time we find ourselves mustering the courage to challenge the status quo, know there is a universe of women standing behind us. We believe you, we understand you, and together we deserve to resist and declare, "No, my place."

- *The founders of Illinois Say No More*

ACKNOWLEDGEMENTS

Working on this book project helped me more fully realize the talented, collaborative and supportive community of Illinois women that is working so hard in government and politics every day.

A thank you is due to so many of them, for their bravery in speaking out about difficult experiences with the hope of ultimately driving change.

Thank you, especially, to Ellie Bahrmasel and Aviva Bowen for help planning and copy editing, and to the family and friends who have shown such love and loyalty in recent months.

ABOUT THE AUTHOR

Kerry Lester is a journalist and author who has reported for the *Associated Press, Daily Herald* and *Chicago Catholic.*

Kerry's been repeatedly named one of the Best State Capitol Reporters in America by the *Washington Post.* She has received awards from the Chicago Journalists Association, Chicago Headline Club and Inland Press Association. Kerry's investigative reporting has also prompted several changes to Illinois state law.

She lives in Chicago.

ABOUT THE ILLUSTRATOR

Pat Byrnes is a Chicago-based cartoonist for *The New Yorker*, with two published anthologies of his works, *What Would Satan Do?* and *Because I'm the Child Here and I Said So.* He is the author of *Captain Dad: The Manly Art of Stay-at-Home Fatherhood*, illustrator of *Eats Shoots & Leaves Illustrated Edition*, and inventor of the patented Smurks® emotional index.

Made in the USA
San Bernardino, CA
03 February 2018